Out and About at the Zoo

Field Trips

Written by Kathleen W. Deady • Illustrated by Anne McMullen

Content Advisor: Larry Killmar
General Curator, San Diego Zoo, San Diego, California

Reading Advisor: Lauren A. Liang, M.A.
Literacy Education, University of Minnesota, Minneapolis, Minnesota

PICTURE WINDOW BOOKS
Minneapolis, Minnesota

To my writing group and dear friends, Muriel, Sally, Jane, Barbara, Diane, Jennifer, Andrea, Mary Jo, and Janet —K.W.D.

The author wishes to thank Larry Killmar, general curator of the San Diego Zoo, and Julie Moore, licensing manager, for their assistance.

Designer: Melissa Voda
Page production: Picture Window Books
The illustrations in this book were rendered using watercolor and ink.

Picture Window Books
5115 Excelsior Boulevard
Suite 232
Minneapolis, MN 55416
1-877-845-8392
www.picturewindowbooks.com

Printed in the United States of America.
1 2 3 4 5 6 08 07 06 05 04 03

Library of Congress Cataloging-in-Publication Data
Deady, Kathleen W.
  Out and about at the zoo / written by Kathleen W. Deady ; illustrated by Anne McMullen.
    p. cm.
  Summary: Uses a field trip to the zoo to introduce various zoo animals, their habitats and how they are recreated, and their care.
  ISBN 1-4048-0041-7 (lib. bdg. : alk. paper)
  1. Zoos—Juvenile literature. 2. Zoo animals—Juvenile literature. [1. Zoos.
2. Zoo animals.] I. McMullen, Anne, ill. II. Title.
  QL76 .D43 2003
  590'.7'3—dc21
                                                                2002006286

We're going on a field trip to the zoo. We can't wait!

Things to find out:
Who takes care of the animals?
What happens if an animal gets sick?
Can we feed and pet the animals?
How do zoos keep visitors safe?

3

Welcome to Wildlife World. Like many new zoos, we have built natural animal homes, or habitats. We want our animals to feel comfortable and move freely. Our first stop today looks like the grasslands of Africa. Don't worry about the lions. We have hidden fences. They keep both you and the animals safe.

4

Let's go into our rain forest habitat. In the wild, animals spend hours looking for food, so zookeepers often hide food for them to find. Food may be hung from trees or spread on the ground. We want the animals to find food in a way that is natural for them.

6

Special machines make the air misty in a zoo's rain forest habitat.
A clear roof lets in sunlight. This helps real rain forest plants and
animals live together, just as they do in the wild.

7

Can you feel how hot and dry the air is here?
It feels like a real desert. Workers can control the
temperature day and night. It's just right for the
animals and plants that live in this desert habitat.

8

Wild animals can get bored in zoos, so zookeepers change things to make habitats look new and interesting. This helps the animals stay alert, active, and healthy.

9

We have all our bears here in Bear Country.
Giant pandas need warm air and lots of bamboo trees.
Polar bears need cold air, ice, and a place to swim.

11

Zoos sometimes group animals together according to where they live in the wild. These animals, for example, all come from Australia. Since they are used to living near each other in the wild, they can live peacefully near each other in the zoo, too.

Zookeepers pay close attention to the animals. If a zookeeper notices that an animal doesn't act right or has stopped eating, they call the zoo doctor.

If our animals get sick or hurt, we bring them here to our
hospital. Zoo doctors are veterinarians. They find out what
is wrong with sick animals and help the animals get well.

14 They also check each animal regularly to make sure it's healthy.

Some animals need help learning to be good mothers.
Zookeepers help them feed and care for their babies.

15

Feeding the animals is a big job. Different animals need different kinds of food. Our kitchen has many things you would find in your own kitchen, such as meat, milk, eggs, fruit, and vegetables. For animals with different needs, we also have leaves, twigs, rats, mice, and insects.

Zookeepers give animals only good, healthy food. That's why zoos have signs that say "Do Not Feed the Animals." Popcorn, peanuts, candies, and other foods that people eat could kill a wild animal or make it sick.

17

Our last stop today is our children's zoo.
Here you can see lots of animals up close
and pet some of them. Our zookeepers
sometimes put on special shows here, too.

Always ask a zookeeper, or read the posted signs, before touching or petting zoo animals. Baby animals need to be treated gently. Some animals, like certain snakes or rodents, should be petted or rubbed in only one direction. Other creatures, like owls or eagles, may be frightened by a human's touch.

We hope you liked learning about our animals and the zoo.
Come back often. There are always new animals to see
at Wildlife World.

MAKE YOUR OWN ZOO MAP

What you need

a large sheet of paper

a pencil

crayons or markers

scissors, glue, and old magazines (optional)

What you do

1. Think about animals you would like to have in your own zoo.

2. Decide how to group your animals.

3. Draw some big shapes on your sheet of paper. Each shape will be an area for a group of animals. Give each area a name, if you like (for example, Bear Country or Desert World).

4. Draw some plants, rocks, or water to make each habitat look natural.

5. Add the animals that go together in each area. You can draw the animals, or glue in pictures that you cut from a magazine.

6. Draw paths from one zoo area to another.

7. You might want to add benches, food stands, and zookeepers. Don't forget the visitors. You have a busy zoo!

FUN FACTS

- One of the first zoos was created in Egypt about 3,500 years ago. This zoo probably had birds, lions, giraffes, monkeys, bears, and elephants.

- Europe had small public zoos as early as the year 900. Kings and queens owned their own private zoos and exchanged animals back and forth like trading cards.

- Carl Hagenbeck, a German circus trainer, is called the "father of the modern zoo." His zoo, which opened in 1907, did not exhibit animals in cages. Hagenbeck built habitats for the animals that were like their own homes in the wild.

- Today there are more than 800 zoos in over 80 countries. The United States has the most zoos, with almost 200. More than 100 million people visit zoos every year in the United States and Canada.

- Some animals hide in the day and come out only at night. In order for their visitors to still see these animals, some zoos have created special displays. At night, the display lights are kept on. The animals think it is daytime and go to sleep. Then during the day, the display is kept dark. The animals think it is nighttime and stay awake and active when visitors can see them.

- The Los Angeles Zoo and the San Diego Wild Animal Park are working together to save the California condor. This huge bird is in danger of dying out forever. The two zoos breed condors and release some of them back into the wild.

- Golden lion tamarins are also endangered. Tamarins are small monkeys from South America. Since 1984, zoos have released more than 140 tamarins back into the wild.

WORDS TO KNOW

desert—a dry place that gets very little rain

endangered—in danger of dying out forever

habitat—the place or area where an animal lives. A habitat is determined by the amount of rain or snow it gets, how hot or cold it is, and what kinds of plants and animals live there.

rain forest—a rainy area with many huge trees and plants

veterinarian—a doctor who takes care of animals

zookeeper—a person who takes care of the daily needs of animals in a zoo

TO LEARN MORE

At the Library

Capucilli, Alyssa Satin. *Inside a Zoo in the City: A Rebus Read–Along Story.* New York: Scholastic, 2000.

Fowler, Allan. *Animals in the Zoo.* New York: Children's Press, 2000.

Massie, Diane Redfield. *The Baby Beebee Bird.* New York: HarperCollins Publishers, 2000.

Nayer, Judy. *Adding It Up at the Zoo.* Mankato, Minn.: Yellow Umbrella Books, 2002.

On the Web

Lincoln Park Zoo

http://www.lpzoo.com

Learn about the animals and activities at Chicago's Lincoln Park Zoo.

Virtual Zoo

http://library.thinkquest.org/11922

Visit an online zoo to find out about animals and how to protect them.

Want to learn more about zoos? Visit FACT HOUND at *http://www.facthound.com.*

INDEX